CREATIVE
EMBELLISHMENTS

Sherrill Kahn

CREATIVE EM

For Paper, Jewelry, Fabric, and More

BELLISHMENTS

Martingale®
& C O M P A N Y

Creative Embellishments: For Paper, Jewelry, Fabric, and More
© 2007 by Sherrill Kahn

Martingale®
& COMPANY

Martingale & Company
20205 144th Ave. NE
Woodinville, WA 98072-8478 USA
www.martingale-pub.com

Printed in China
12 11 10 09 08 07   8 7 6 5 4

Library of Congress Cataloging-in-Publication Data
Library of Congress Control Number: 2006026577

ISBN: 978-1-56477-616-7

mission statement

Dedicated to providing quality products and service to inspire creativity.

credits

CEO:	Tom Wierzbicki
Publisher:	Jane Hamada
Editorial Director:	Mary V. Green
Managing Editor:	Tina Cook
Technical Editor:	Dawn Anderson
Copy Editor:	Melissa Bryan
Design Director:	Stan Green
Cover and Text Designer:	Stan Green
Photographer:	Brent Kane

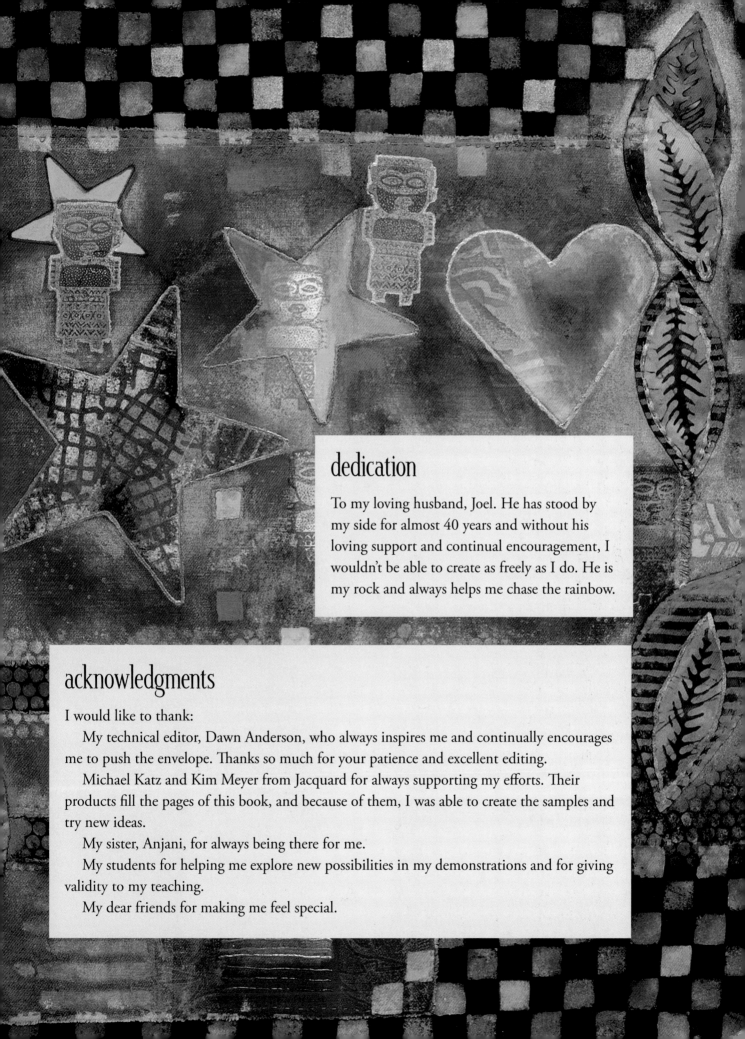

dedication

To my loving husband, Joel. He has stood by my side for almost 40 years and without his loving support and continual encouragement, I wouldn't be able to create as freely as I do. He is my rock and always helps me chase the rainbow.

acknowledgments

I would like to thank:

My technical editor, Dawn Anderson, who always inspires me and continually encourages me to push the envelope. Thanks so much for your patience and excellent editing.

Michael Katz and Kim Meyer from Jacquard for always supporting my efforts. Their products fill the pages of this book, and because of them, I was able to create the samples and try new ideas.

My sister, Anjani, for always being there for me.

My students for helping me explore new possibilities in my demonstrations and for giving validity to my teaching.

My dear friends for making me feel special.

CONTENTS

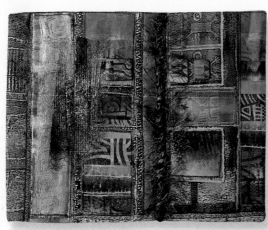

INTRODUCTION

When writing this book, I wanted to include every technique I've ever learned. That just wasn't possible. For everything that has been included in this book, there is just as much that has been left out. And of course I am always learning new things. That is the nature of creativity. A sound, a sight, and a scene can all cause a creative spark. New and constantly evolving products also make me want to explore the possibilities.

In this book, I share techniques that can be used for embellishing all kinds of projects. These techniques use a variety of materials, including paint, fabric, paper, clay, beads, shrink plastic, decorative yarns, and much more. If you enjoy creating, whether it be through painting, paper crafts, quilting, scrapbooking, jewelry making, garment sewing, or collage, you will find lots of inspiration on the following pages for creatively embellishing your designs.

I am surrounded by a rich environment. My studio is filled with color and texture, a variety of supplies and tools, and hundreds of books. I also notice things in everyday life that could possibly turn into my next inspiration. I don't plan my work in advance. I let the project lead to its own fulfillment. I often am led in ways that are completely different than I had originally anticipated.

I visit large warehouse stores of office and home-improvement supplies and walk the aisles looking for items that can be used to make art. Some of my most interesting experiments involve materials not originally designated as art tools.

I keep a very organized studio. I don't go to bed at night until everything is neatly put away or organized for the next day. I keep similar supplies and tools in the same spot so that they are easily found. I also try to organize my books by subject matter. Try to find a spot in your home where you can work easily, even if it's just a table and a portable organizer on wheels. Lighting is essential, so locate your work table where you will have adequate light nearby, as well as water for use in creating projects and cleaning up.

Use this book as a starting point, and don't be afraid to try anything and everything with your art. Live by the phrase "What if?" and let it guide you. Make each moment count and try something new each day. But most of all, have fun!

> Live by the phrase "What if?" and let it guide you. Make each moment count and try something new each day.

TOOLS AND SUPPLIES

This section describes the tools and supplies needed to create the gorgeous painted surfaces and embellishments shown in this book.

For convenience, the items are listed alphabetically in one comprehensive section rather than with each individual project. When reading the directions for a specific technique, refer to this list. You won't need all of these supplies; begin by gathering the materials for the projects that appeal to you most, and add to your collection as your creativity blooms.

- **Air-dry clay.** Air-dry clay can be painted and impressed with various textures. In this book, all samples were made with Hearty air-dry clay.
- **Angelina.** This product looks like cotton candy and is fused together by ironing it between two Teflon sheets.
- **Awls or darning needles.** Use these for punching holes in porous materials.
- **Beads.** I use several types of beads in my projects. I like seed beads in various colors for adding embellishments to most surfaces. Larger beads can be used for making necklaces and jewelry.
- **Bracelet links.** Bracelet links joined with bracelet findings at the ends are great for making jewelry.
- **Brushes.** I use two main brush sizes: a size 2 detail brush for thin lines and a ½"-wide flat brush for broad strokes of color.
- **Buttons.** Use buttons of various sizes and colors for embellishments.

- **Cardboard.** Use thick cardboard as a drawing board when using markers or other dry media. Cardboard can warp if used with wet media.

- **Cardstock.** Use cardstock in a variety of colors as a base for painting, rubber-stamping, and even sewing. I prefer 60#- or 80#-weight paper.

- **Chopsticks.** When painted, these work great for suspending small wall hangings or stiff paper pieces.

- **Cutting mats.** Use a self-healing cutting mat when cutting fabric or paper with rotary cutters.

- **Elastic hair bands.** Small bands work well for wrapping around shrink plastic when creating beads. Medium-sized bands can be used as bases for fabric-wrapped bracelet bands and large ones work well as bases for adding necklace elements. I always head to the hair-accessories aisle when I want to stock up on elastic bands. They come in a wide variety of sizes, and many of the bands today have protective coatings.

- **Fabric.** Use white or black cotton with a high thread count for painting and rubber-stamping fiber projects. Polyester fabric can also be used for painting and rubber-stamping. The color reacts differently on polyester than it does on cotton. Use flannel bed sheeting in place of batting for wall hangings since it lies flat and is easy to stitch through when adding hand- or machine-sewn embellishments. Use commercially printed fabric for embellishing. In this book I used my own fabric designs from Robert Kaufman Fabrics on some of the projects.

- **Freezer paper.** Use freezer paper, shiny side up, to protect your work surface when painting. It also works as an excellent paint palette.

- **Fun foam.** Fun foam works well as a painting surface and can be used to make jewelry and other embellishments. It can also serve as a backing to reinforce lighter-weight materials.

- **Gloss medium.** This product works great for sealing and adding shine to a design surface.

Jacquard's Pearl Ex varnish may be used in place of gloss medium.

- **Glue.** Some of my favorite glue products, listed here, are all made by Crafter's Pick. The Ultimate! adhesive is great for gluing difficult and heavy items to a design surface. Memory Mount works well for gluing paper, and Fabric Glue is designed for bonding fabric pieces together without sewing.

- **Hammer.** Use a hammer for flattening items and for nailing pieces together.

- **Heat gun.** Ranger's Heat it Craft Tool has a large nozzle for heating shrink plastic and drying wet painted pieces.

- **Hole punches.** Use a ¼" punch for making larger holes in various surfaces. Use a ⅛" punch for medium holes and a ¹⁄₁₆" punch for making small holes in buttons and jewelry dangles.

- **Illustration board and mat board.** These boards can be used for mounting creative projects. Illustration board is very smooth and is a better choice for collage projects.

- **Iron.** Use an iron for pressing projects flat.

- **Ironing board.** Use an ironing board with a padded cover when applying heat from an iron to projects. Be sure the cover is in good condition.

- **Knitting needle.** Use metal knitting needles as an aid when creating shrink plastic beads—and also, of course, for knitting.

- **Markers.** Use Sharpie permanent markers with fine and ultra-fine tips for adding waterproof details to projects.

- **Metal sheets.** Thin copper metal or colored metals make nice embellishments for projects. These thin metals can be embossed with designs for a textural effect.

- **Needles.** Hand-sewing needles are needed for adding stitches to fabric and paper projects. For machine sewing, use a needle appropriate for the thread type used in your sewing machine.

- **Paint.** Jacquard's Textile Color, Neopaque, Lumiere, Dye-na-Flow, and Sherrill's Sorbets are great paints for flexibility in layering colors on porous creative projects.
- **Paper.** Use paper of your choice for the pages in a stapled book. Save painted scraps of paper to use in collages.
- **Paper brads.** These tiny brads can be used for embellishment in all projects that involve hole punches.
- **Paper towels.** Use paper towels for cleanup when using messy supplies.
- **Pencil.** Use a pencil for marking and drawing on dry surfaces.
- **Piñata Colors.** These paints from Jacquard are for use on nonporous surfaces.
- **Pin backs.** These are needed for turning embellishments into wearable pins and brooches.
- **Pipe cleaners.** Chenille pipe cleaners in the colors of your choice can be wrapped with fabric and yarn to create embellishments for most surfaces.
- **Plastic knife.** This type of knife, such as you get with takeout food, works well for toothbrush spattering.
- **Plastic sheet.** Use a plastic sheet to protect your work surface when using messy materials.
- **Plastic sheet protectors.** Sandwich collage pieces between the layers of sheet protectors and fuse them together to make embellishments.
- **Pot holder.** Use a pot holder to hold hot projects, including those that involve grasping metal knitting needles and applying heat from a heat gun. Shrink plastic and sheet protector beads are formed around metal knitting needles. The needles become quite hot during the heating process.
- **Rotary cutters.** Use rotary cutters for cutting fabric and paper on a self-healing cutting mat.

- **Rubber stamps.** Rubber stamps can be used for adding texture and designs to creative projects. All the stamps used in this book are from Impress Me rubber stamps.
- **Rubbing plates.** These plastic plates are used to make marker rubbings on fabric.
- **Ruler.** A metal-edged ruler is helpful when cutting paper with an X-Acto knife.
- **Scissors.** You may need both cloth and paper scissors.

- **Scraper.** An old credit card makes a great scraper for removing paint. You can also purchase scrapers for this purpose in various sizes.
- **Sequin waste.** This product comes in various sizes and can be found at floral-supply stores. I use it for stenciling.
- **Sewing machine.** I used the Janome Jem Platinum and Janome Memory Craft 10001 for all the machine sewing in this book. I found that I got perfect stitches whether combining paper and silk, or various layers of fiber and paper.
- **Shrink plastic.** Use shrink plastic for making buttons, beads, and embellishments. I prefer Lucky Squirrel brand.
- **Sponge squares.** Use sponge squares for applying paint to rubber stamps and to a design surface.
- **Spray bottle.** Use a fine-mist spray bottle for dampening the design surface when working with wet techniques.
- **Stamp pad reinkers.** Stamp pad reinkers are used to add ink to dry stamp pads.
- **Stamp pads.** Clearsnap Chalks, Ancient Page, and Crafter stamp pads work well on various design surfaces. The ink can be brushed, stamped, and sponged onto the surfaces. Jacquard's Pearl Ex stamp pads work on nonporous surfaces.
- **Stapler.** Use a stapler with a deep throat for binding books.
- **Stencil brushes.** Stencil brushes are used to apply paint through stencil openings. Style Stone Inking Brushes from Clearsnap are quite small and are essential for stenciling through small stencil openings or for adding tiny details to three-dimensional projects.
- **Stencils.** A stencil can be any flat item with an opening through which paint can be applied. Stenciled impressions can be made in any shape and size.

- **Stuffing tool.** Whether you use a commercial tool or you make one as I describe on page 38 in step 9, this item is quite handy for stuffing fabric shapes.
- **Tape.** Use double-stick tape for securing pieces of paper together. Use paper tape to secure stencils in place when stenciling on paper.
- **Teflon ironing sheets.** You'll need two Teflon ironing sheets for heat setting and for making three-dimensional pieces from Tyvek or shrink plastic.
- **Thread.** You'll need sewing thread for machine stitching and for embellishing porous surfaces.
- **Tiles.** Use an unglazed tile from a tile supplier or large home-improvement store to protect the work surface when using a heating tool. Tiles can also be used as design surfaces.
- **Toothbrush.** Use a battery-operated rotary toothbrush for cleaning rubber stamps and for applying paint to a design surface. It also works great for stenciling techniques. Use a regular toothbrush for spattering paint.
- **Tyvek envelopes.** Cut pieces from Tyvek envelopes and press them between Teflon ironing sheets to create textured embellishments.
- **Water containers.** You'll need at least two for holding water when painting.
- **Wire.** Use 24-gauge or 26-gauge wire for making wire beads.
- **Wire cutters.** Wire cutters or old scissors are needed for cutting fine-gauge craft wire.
- **Wooden shapes.** Paint small wooden shapes and use them as embellishments.
- **Wood molding.** Use right-angle wood molding for hanging wall hangings. Paint the molding to coordinate with your project.
- **X-Acto knife.** Use for cutting paper on a self-healing mat.

- **Xyron laminating machine.** Use this machine to make laminated pieces.
- **Yarn.** Decorative yarns, cords, and threads are used for making wrapped chenille pipe cleaners. They can also serve a variety of other functions when making embellishments.

CREATING SERENDIPITY FABRIC OR PAPER

Serendipity fabric or paper is a happy by-product of the creative process. Keep a scrap piece of fabric or paper near your design surface where you can brush, sponge, roll, or pat off the excess paint from the tool you're using. Add to the fabric or paper as you do each project. You never know; you may end up with a fabulous piece without even trying. Allow the serendipity piece to dry and use it in a future project.

PAINTING AND RUBBER-STAMPING TECHNIQUES

This section covers painting techniques using many different tools and mediums. You will also find thorough step-by-step instructions for creative rubber stamping with a variety of tools, inks, and paints.

Painting with a Paintbrush

Each style of paintbrush produces a unique effect.

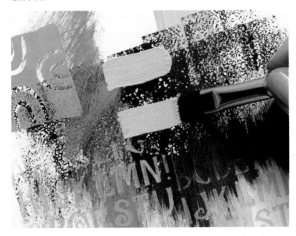

Use a flat brush to apply broad areas of color to the design surface.

Use a size 2 detail brush to produce narrow painted lines or to outline or highlight specific areas of a design.

Dry Brushing

This technique is especially useful for coloring embellishment pieces.

1. Dip the brush into thick paint, such as Neopaque.
2. Remove most of the paint onto a serendipity piece.
3. With the nearly dry brush, apply the paint to the chosen design surface. You can use a sweeping side motion (shown below), or keep the brush perpendicular to the surface.

Using Applicator-Tipped Paint

1. Apply a metal tip to an applicator-tipped bottle, such as Lumiere, Neopaque, Textile Colors, or Sherrill's Sorbets by Jacquard.
2. Squeeze the bottle gently to apply paint to the design surface, using it to highlight and add texture to selected areas. Always test the bottle on a serendipity piece before applying the paint, since the tip could become clogged.

Sponge Painting Backgrounds

Apply the paint type of your choice to a sponge square and pat the sponge onto a dry surface to create a colored background.

Dry Sponging

This technique works well when used over a previously stamped design.

1. Squeeze any type of paint onto a sponge square and pat off most of the paint onto a serendipity piece.
2. When the sponge is no longer shiny with paint, apply the paint in light layers over the design surface.

Glazing with Textile Colors

Textile Color paints can be used on both fabric and paper. Squeeze your chosen shade of Jacquard's Textile Color onto a sponge square and sponge the paint over the selected area of your design. Textile Colors are transparent, making them ideal for multiple paint layers.

Applying Paint to a Wet Surface

1. Spray the design surface with water from a spray bottle.
2. Apply wet color to the surface with a sponge or squeeze bottle. The paint will flow on the wet surface and mix together where the colors touch, creating a second color, or even a third color. Many types of products work well for this technique, including Jacquard's Dye-na-Flow, all inks, all liquid dyes, and any other liquid paint, including watercolors.

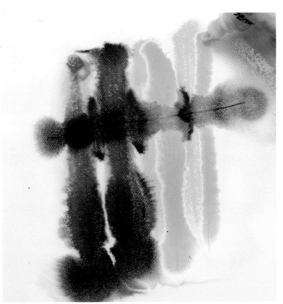

Creating Salt Designs

1. Follow the steps for "Applying Paint to a Wet Surface" (left).
2. Sprinkle rock salt or other salt onto the wet surface to create interesting effects.

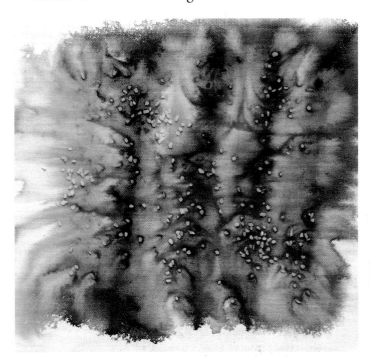

3. Let the paint dry and then brush away the salt.

Painting with a Rotary Toothbrush

This is a wonderful way to add texture to a project.

1. Dip a rotary toothbrush into the paint of your choice, but avoid alcohol-based paints because they dry quickly.
2. Turn on the toothbrush and remove any excess paint onto a serendipity piece.
3. Apply the paint to the design surface with the toothbrush.

Toothbrush Spattering

This technique can be used through stencil openings to create an airbrushed effect.

1. Dip a toothbrush into the paint of your choice, but avoid alcohol-based paint. Remove any excess onto a serendipity piece.
2. To spatter the paint, run the toothbrush across the edge of a disposable plastic knife, toward the design surface.

ROTARY-TOOTHBRUSH PAINTING WITH STENCILS

Rotary-toothbrush painting works well for applying paint in the tiny openings of a stencil, especially small brass stencils.

Using Colored Pencils

Draw onto the design surface with colored pencils, building up layers of colors.

Using Water-Soluble Colored Pencils

1. Draw onto the design surface with water-soluble colored pencils, building up layers of colors.

2. Spray the colored surface with a mist of water from a spray bottle, to create a watercolor effect (shown bottom left).

Scraping Paint

This technique works best on fabric with a high thread count and on paper with a smooth surface.

1. Squeeze paint onto the design surface. I like to use Jacquard's Textile Colors for this first step. They work great on fabric and smooth porous surfaces, acting as a sealer.

2. Scrape through the paint with a flat plastic tool such as an old credit card or other scraping tool.

Rubber-Stamping with Paint: Making a Single Impression

1. Squeeze one or more paint colors onto a sponge square.
2. Pat the color onto the stamp.
3. Press the stamp onto the desired surface.
4. Repeat steps 2 and 3 to achieve the desired results.

Rubber-Stamping with Paint: Making Multiple Partial Impressions

This technique allows you to create a series of stamped images in a spontaneous manner.

1. Squeeze one or more paint colors onto a sponge square.
2. Press the edge of a stamp onto the sponge.
3. Press the edge of the stamp onto the desired surface.
4. Repeat steps 2 and 3 to achieve the desired results.

USE SHERRILL'S SORBETS TO CREATE LAYERS OF RUBBER-STAMPED COLORS

Sherrill's Sorbets paints are extremely opaque, so they can be used with rubber stamps to apply color over previous layers of paint and will give a crisp, clean stamped image.

Rubber-Stamping with Stamp Pads

1. Pat the stamp pad onto the stamp.
2. Press the stamp onto the desired surface.

Using Stamp Pads to Apply Color Directly to the Design Surface

Use stamp pads to pat ink onto the design surface, making single impressions or overlapping patterns.

Using a Sponge to Apply Stamp Pad Ink to the Design Surface

Dab a sponge onto the surface of the ink pad to pick up color, and then sponge the color onto the design surface. Clearsnap Chalk, Ancient Page, and Crafter stamp pads are all recommended.

Stamping with Pearl Ex Stamp Pad Inks

The following steps involve stamping on non-porous surfaces.

1. Pat a rubber stamp on the stamp pad, loading it with ink.
2. Press the stamp onto the desired surface very carefully so that you do not smear the ink.
3. Heat set the ink with a heat tool.

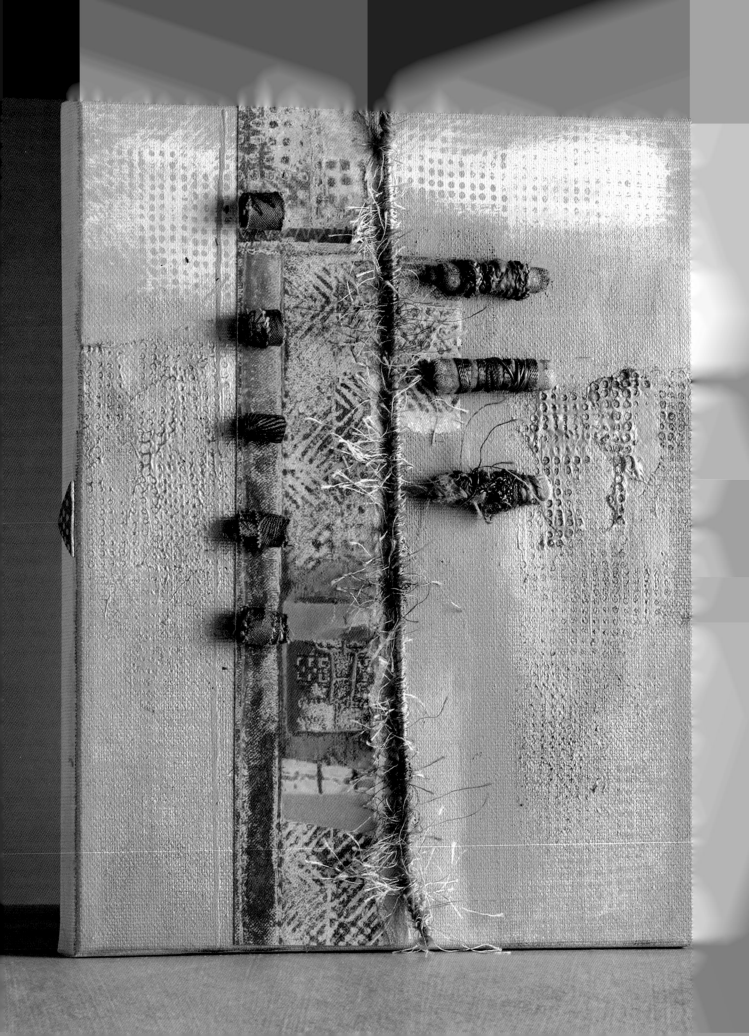

FABRIC AND PAPER BEADS

This section offers several techniques for making fabric and paper beads. These beads are easy to make, and they look dramatic when used to create jewelry or to embellish projects such as wall hangings, cards, or journals.

Fabric or Paper Beads from Drinking Straws

1. Apply Crafter's Pick The Ultimate! adhesive to the end of a strip of fabric or paper for about 1". Cut a straw to the desired length and place it in the glue.
2. Roll the fabric or paper around the straw and trim the excess. Make a clean cut on the ends of the covered straw, if desired. Cut the straw into beads of the desired length.
3. Embellish the beads, if desired, using one of the methods on page 26.

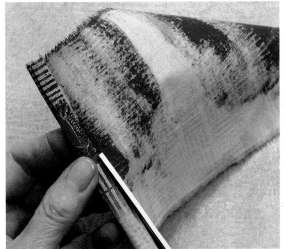

Canvas Panel Collage with Fabric Beads and a Wrapped Pipe Cleaner

An 8" x 10" piece of stretched canvas was painted with various paints and textured with molding paste and rubber stamps. The textured area was accented with layers of Lumiere. A computer-generated collage was glued to the left side of the piece. The design is given a more substantial, dimensional quality with the addition of several wrapped fabric beads and a wrapped pipe-cleaner embellishment. A picture hanger attached to the center back makes this piece suitable for hanging.

Yarn and fibers. Wrap yarn or other fibers around the drinking-straw bead, securing the ends in place with glue (above).

Wire and seed beads. String seed beads onto 24-gauge, 26-gauge, or 28-gauge wire. Don't cut the wire from the spool (left).

Place 1" of the wire along the length of the straw bead, and then wrap the wire around the end of the bead three or four times. Ease the beads down the wire and wrap around the straw bead. Wrap the wire three or four more times around the straw bead. Trim off the excess wire and secure the end with a dot of glue. See photos below.

Paper-Towel Beads

1. Tear paper toweling into small strips about 1¼"-wide.

2. Apply various paint colors to the paper strips and let dry.

3. Brush gloss medium or Jacquard's Pearl Ex varnish on both sides of a strip.

4. Roll the wet paper-towel strip around a metal knitting needle.

5. Scrunch the wet paper toweling around the knitting needle.

6. Remove immediately and place on a piece of freezer paper to dry.

More Ideas

Paper towel beads can be thick or thin and can be painted a variety of colors.

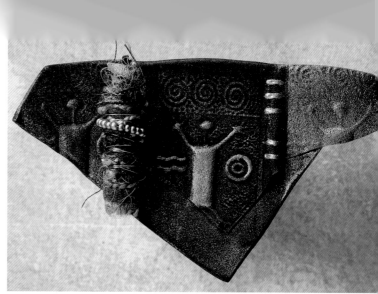

Fun-Foam Pin

Fun foam was heated, textured with a rubber stamp, and then painted to create this stunning design. The piece was further accented with a fabric bead encircled by wire and seed beads. A pin back was glued to the design to turn it into a piece of jewelry.

Standing Cardstock Doll with Air-Dry Clay Face and Fabric-Bead Necklace

A doll image, rubber-stamped on cardstock, is accented with dry sponging and colored pencils. The doll features a face of air-dry clay, a beaded necklace, and a fabric bead as an accent. The doll is reinforced with cardstock and has a cardstock stand to keep it upright. See detail at right.

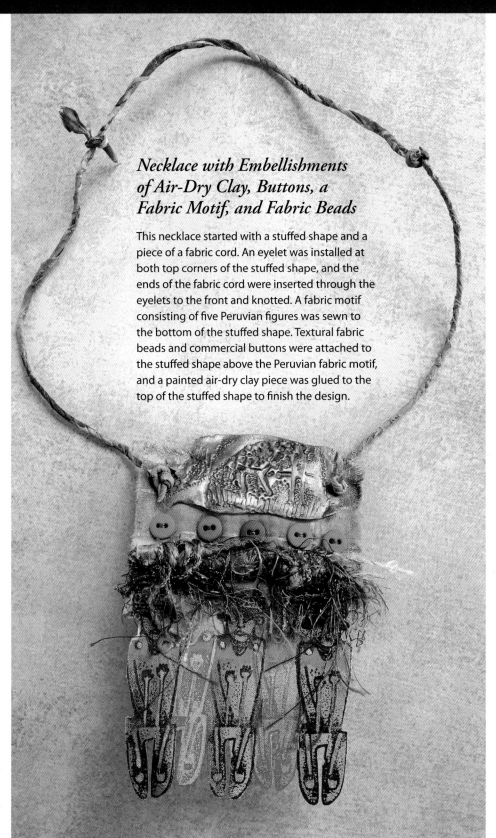

Necklace with Embellishments of Air-Dry Clay, Buttons, a Fabric Motif, and Fabric Beads

This necklace started with a stuffed shape and a piece of a fabric cord. An eyelet was installed at both top corners of the stuffed shape, and the ends of the fabric cord were inserted through the eyelets to the front and knotted. A fabric motif consisting of five Peruvian figures was sewn to the bottom of the stuffed shape. Textural fabric beads and commercial buttons were attached to the stuffed shape above the Peruvian fabric motif, and a painted air-dry clay piece was glued to the top of the stuffed shape to finish the design.

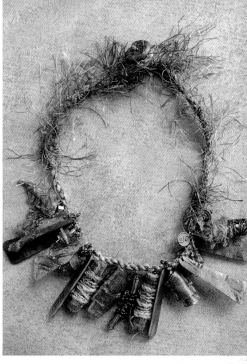

Necklace with Fabric Beads, Shrink-Plastic Dangles, and Wire Beads

The accents on this necklace are attached to a crocheted chain that was created with textural yarn. The back fastens by means of a button and buttonhole closure. A variety of fabric beads, shrink-plastic beads and dangles, and a wire bead are attached to the center front of the crocheted chain. See detail below.

AIR-DRY CLAY EMBELLISHMENTS

There are a variety of air-dry clays on the market and each has different properties. Experiment with them to decide which you like best. Right now I am using Hearty clays. Hearty makes a translucent polymer air-dry clay called Lumina. I love working with it because the paints and dyes glow on the surface and it can be formed into very thin sheets. The distributor of Lumina and Hearty, a company called The Mountain Idea, has an incredible clay-roller system with four height settings. One of the settings allows you to roll a very thin layer of clay, which I especially enjoy when using Lumina clay.

Hand-Pressed Clay Embellishments with Stamped Impressions

1. Form clay into a ball of the desired size.
2. Roll the ball in your hands and then flatten it to a ¼" thickness.
3. Shape the clay into a circle, oval, square, or other desired shape, using your hands or a plastic knife.
4. Press a deeply etched rubber stamp into the clay. I used Impress Me rubber stamps for projects throughout the book. They are unmounted, making them easier to remove from the clay.
5. If the clay protrudes beyond the edges of the stamp, add other stamped designs around the edges if desired. After stamping into the clay, roll the stamp off of the clay in a gentle motion so that the impression remains intact.
6. Let the clay dry until it hardens.
7. Decorate the clay with paints of your choice and by using dry-brushing techniques. (See "Dry Brushing" on page 17.)

Mini Wall Hanging with Embellishments of Rubber-Stamping, Machine-Appliqué, and Air-Dry Clay

Fabric is embellished with paint and rubber-stamping and features appliqué designs layered with rubber-stamped images. Air-dry clay embellishments are glued to the wall hanging for dimensional interest.

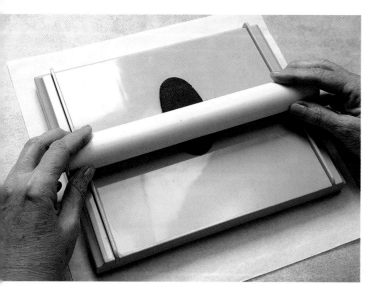

Using a Roller System to Make Clay Embellishments with Stamped Impressions

1. Mix Lumina with a colored clay, and then roll it flat using a clay roller system.
2. Gently remove the clay from the bed of the roller system so it remains intact. Place the clay, shiny side up, on a piece of freezer paper. Use a plastic knife to cut the clay into the desired shape.
3. Follow step 4 on page 31.
4. Follow steps 5–7 on page 31, allowing the clay to dry overnight before painting.

USING DYE-NA-FLOW ON LUMINA AIR-DRY CLAY EMBELLISHMENTS

Using only Lumina clay, follow steps 1–3 of "Using a Roller System to Make Clay Embellishments with Stamped Impressions." While the clay is still wet, brush Dye-na-Flow onto the surface, letting the colors mix together.

Let the clay dry overnight. Glaze the embellishment with gloss medium or Pearl Ex varnish. Add metallic highlights with dry-brushing techniques.

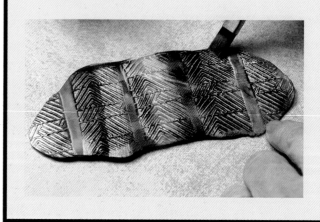

Air-Dry Clay Beads

You can take two different approaches to making air-dry clay beads.

Stamped air-dry clay beads. Follow the general instructions for "Hand-Pressed Clay Embellishments with Stamped Impressions" on page 31 or "Using a Roller System to Make Clay Embellishments with Stamped Impressions" on page 32. Before drying, trim the clay to the desired size and roll it around a metal knitting needle. Roll the needle and slip the bead off. Allow to dry and paint as desired.

Round air-dry clay beads. Roll a piece of clay into a round ball. Push a needle or toothpick through the center to create a hole. Rock the needle or toothpick back and forth to remove it from the clay. Allow to dry and paint as desired.

AIR-DRY CLAY GALLERY

Rubber-Stamped Pins

These three pins were created by pressing rubber stamps into air-dry clay. The designs were painted with various colors of Lumiere. A pin back was glued to each of the finished designs.

Tall Glass Bottle Embellished with an Air-Dry Clay Piece

To create the depth and richness apparent in this design, Neopaque was poured inside a glass bottle. With the cork in place, the bottle was shaken to coat the inside of the bottle with paint, and then the paint was poured out. Rubber-stamped designs were added to the outside of the bottle with Pearl Ex stamp pads. The designs were heat set between applications. A painted air-dry clay piece with a stamped design was glued to the top of the bottle to create a focal point. The bottle became a vase for a floral arrangement.

Wall Plaque with Large Clay Piece

A 7" square of wood, painted and stamped with Lumiere and Neopaque, serves as the base of this wall plaque. A ⅜"-thick free-form air-dry clay piece with stamped designs was painted and glued to the wood base. For more textural interest, a wrapped pipe cleaner was glued over the clay design.

Air-Dry Clay Necklace with Dangles

The base of this air-dry clay necklace is made from a crocheted chain that has a button and buttonhole closure at the back. Several air-dry clay dangles were created by stamping designs in flattened clay pieces and painting them. One or two holes were made in each dangle with a toothpick so that they could be attached to the crocheted chain. Additional metal charms and assorted beads were added to the necklace for variety.

STUFFED SHAPES

Stuffed shapes make wonderful embellishments, or they can be the stars of a project, especially when those shapes are dolls or animals. Embellishing stuffed shapes with beads, buttons, surface embroidery, machine embroidery, ribbons, yarns, metal shapes, dangles, or whatever the mind imagines is a wonderful experience.

Creating Stuffed Shapes

1. Paint or stamp an image (such as a doll, bead, animal, or abstract shape) onto fabric. Decorate a second piece of fabric about the same size as the first to use as the backing.
2. Pin the two pieces of fabric wrong sides together.
3. Sew around the edges of the stamped image using a short stitch length on the sewing machine. You may also stitch by hand, if desired.
4. Add paint to the stamped design. For transparent color, use Jacquard Textile Colors.
5. Use a flat brush to paint a border about ¼" wide around the sewn edge of the image on both sides of the stitched fabric. I use Sherrill's Sorbets or Neopaque by Jacquard for the border.
6. Let the paint dry, and then trim ⅛" from the stitching line with sharp sewing scissors, leaving an approximately ⅛"-wide painted border on the edges. See top-left photo on page 38.

Stuffed Painted Doll

The outline of this doll shape was drawn with permanent markers on plain white cotton fabric. Paint was applied over the surface with sponging, stenciling, and stamping. The doll image was stitched to a background fabric, then stuffed and trimmed. Paint, seed beads, and a charm were added for extra embellishment.

7. Add more color to the design if desired.

8. To stuff the shape, use a very sharp pair of scissors to cut slits in the back layer of fabric. Be careful not to cut through to the front layer of fabric. If you do, you can cover your mistake with embellishments.

9. Use a stuffing tool and fiberfill to stuff the shape (below left). I make my own stuffing tool out of a piece of 16-gauge wire: I simply flatten the ends of the wire with a hammer and then file the ends smooth.

10. Glue embellishments such as small fabric motifs (see "Paper and Fabric Motifs" on page 89) over the slits on the back of the stuffed shape.

11. Decorate the stuffed shape with selected embellishments such as beads, dangles, Angelina, buttons, or thread, if desired.

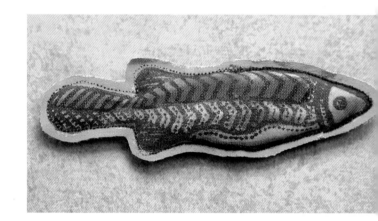

CREATING FRAYED EDGES ON A STUFFED SHAPE

Skip steps 5 and 6 of "Creating Stuffed Shapes" on page 37 and instead paint a wash of color on the edges. Let the design dry, trim ³⁄₁₆" from the stitching line, and then pull loose threads from the edges to ravel them, creating an interesting texture.

More Ideas

These stuffed shapes show some of the possibilities using this technique.

STUFFED-SHAPES GALLERY

Necklace with Doll and Air-Dry Clay Piece on Ultrasuede

A stuffed doll design and a large air-dry clay piece are the focal points of this necklace. Four holes were pierced on the clay piece before the clay dried so that seed beads could be strung across the piece between the holes. The clay and doll accents were hand stitched to a strip of heavy Ultrasuede that was sponged with Lumiere. A loop was created at one end of the Ultrasuede strip and a knot was made at the other end to create a closure for the necklace.

Necklace with Stuffed Mask and Triangular Stuffed Shapes

Six rubber-stamped triangular stuffed shapes and a rubber-stamped stuffed mask were sewn to a colorful crocheted cord. Each shape was painted with Lumiere, Neopaque, and Sherrill's Sorbets. The triangle shapes received some dimensional interest by the addition of seed beads that were stitched to the top of each triangle as it was sewn to the edge of the crocheted chain.

Stuffed Doll Necklace with Laminated Accents

Crocheted fabric cord serves as the base for attaching several stuffed and laminated shapes. A stuffed doll with a beaded necklace serves as a focal point. A folded flat fabric triangle is attached behind the stuffed and laminated shapes at the center to create a background. A textured Tyvek shape has been sewn to the triangular piece of fabric. A loop in the crocheted cord and a button serve as the closure.

Bracelet with Stuffed Shape

The base of this bracelet is made from a ¼"-diameter elastic hair band that was wrapped with ½"-wide fabric strips. The elastic band was stretched during the wrapping process so that it wouldn't be too tight around the wrist when finished. Seed beads were stitched over the fabric strips for interest. A stuffed shape was stitched to the top of the bracelet and accented on the sides with metal embellishments and square beads.

Stuffed Triangular Pendant

A triangular stuffed shape was made by stitching two triangular pieces of painted and stamped fabric right sides together and then turning the stitched piece right side out and stuffing it. A stuffed figure in the shape of a Peruvian doll is attached to the left side of the triangular pendant, and a painted plastic lizard that has been wrapped with strung seed beads accents the center top. A Tyvek button is attached on the right of the design. The pendant is stitched to a piece of purchased cord that has been painted. A loop was created at one end of the cord and an air-dry clay button was attached at the other end to create the closure for the necklace.

ANGELINA EMBELLISHMENTS

Angelina is a remarkable product that looks a lot like angel hair. It comes in a variety of colors, and it fuses together with heat to create a thin fabric that's sure to produce "oohs" and "aahs" when used in your projects. Use the colors individually or combine them for interesting results. Threads, cords, and yarns can be combined with Angelina to make even more varied designs. Angelina embellishments can be sewn or glued to the design surface.

Plain Angelina Embellishments

1. Place a small amount of Angelina on a Teflon ironing sheet.
2. Lay another Teflon ironing sheet over the Angelina, and iron with a warm iron for a few seconds. Do not overheat.
3. Remove the ironing sheet and use the Angelina as is or cut it to the desired shape.

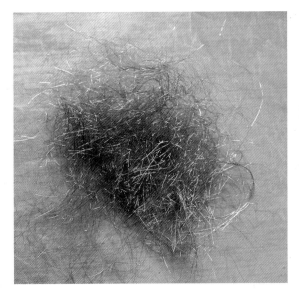

Stretched Canvas Accented with Angelina, Beads, and Metal Pieces

A painted piece of 8" x 10" stretched canvas is the perfect background for layering with embellishments. A vertical collage is glued to the center of the canvas and accented on both sides with pieces of Angelina. Heated metal accents are glued to the upper-left side of the design, and fabric and paper beads are attached to the right of the collage. To finish the piece, an 8" x 10" piece of mat board was glued to the back of the canvas and a sawtooth hanger was nailed near the top.

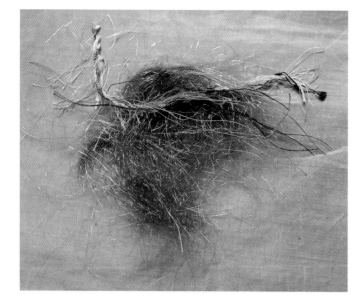

Angelina, Yarn, and Thread Embellishments

1. Place a small amount of Angelina on a Teflon ironing sheet. Weave yarn or threads into the Angelina, or place them on top.
2. Lay another Teflon ironing sheet over the Angelina and iron with a warm iron for a few seconds.
3. Remove the ironing sheet and use the embellishment as is or cut to the desired shape.

Embossed Angelina Embellishments

Follow "Plain Angelina Embellishments," steps 1–3 on page 43, except lay deep-etched unmounted rubber stamps under the Angelina before ironing it. When the stamps are removed, the shape of the stamps will be embossed on the surface of the Angelina. See photos below left and right.

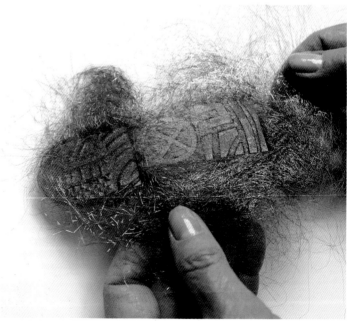

> **SEWING ANGELINA TO A DESIGN SURFACE**
> Place the Angelina on a paper or fabric design surface and sew it in place by hand or with a sewing machine. Metallic thread is the most interesting choice for this purpose, since it complements the surface.

Pleating Angelina Embellishments

1. Follow steps 1–3 for "Plain Angelina Embellishments" on page 43. Pleat the fused Angelina until satisfied with the design (above right).

2. Cover the pleated Angelina with a Teflon ironing sheet and iron until the pleats fuse to one another (right).

> *More Ideas*
> The samples below show a wide variety of color and embossing possibilities with Angelina. Fused Angelina is easily trimmed to create smooth edges rather than fuzzy edges.

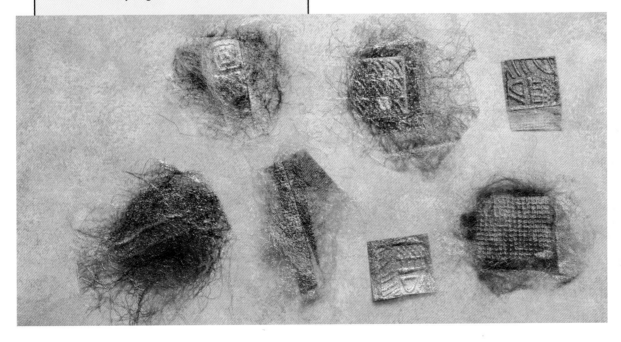

Greeting Card with Angelina Embellishment

This greeting card was created by decorating a piece of glossy cardstock with rubber-stamped impressions using stamp-pad inks. The card was then buffed to achieve a high gloss. The front of the card is accented with Angelina, a wrapped pipe cleaner, and three buttons.

Cardstock Book with Angelina Embellishment and Fabric Beads

The cover of the book was decorated with paint and then accented with an embossed Angelina embellishment and three fabric beads. Then pages were folded and stapled into the book.

Small Embellished Wall Hanging

This piece was created by making two very small painted wall hangings and sewing them together with a tight satin stitch. The finished piece includes a sewn Tyvek embellishment, several shrink-plastic pieces, two wrapped chenille pipe-cleaner pieces, an air-dry clay piece, a fun-foam embellishment, and a piece of chenille pipe cleaner with a Clearsnap Style Stone. A piece of Angelina is glued to the left of the design.

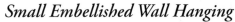

Small Wall Hanging with Accents of Air-Dry Clay, a Wrapped Pipe Cleaner, and Angelina

A small painted wall hanging is embellished with three air-dry clay pieces. An Angelina accent is glued to the left side of the design for interest, and a wrapped chenille pipe cleaner is attached near the center to add a strong vertical line.

METAL EMBELLISHMENTS

Metal makes a wonderful embellishment. Metal and mesh come in a variety of colors and weights and each has special properties. Thin metals and mesh are easy to cut and shape and are inexpensive additions to _____. Wire is also great for embellishing projects and makes wonderful _____ natural-colored metal wire as well as color-coated wire. _____ ovement stores as well as hobby, craft, and rubber-_____ riety of sheet metals, mesh, and wire.

_____ tiny beads onto 24- or _____ re. If desired, add interest _____ beads with dangles or metal shapes made from thin copper. Don't cut the wire from the spool.

2. Place 1" of the end of the wire along the pointed end of a size 3 or smaller knitting needle.

3. Wrap the wire several times around the knitting needle, concealing the wire tail. Keep the beads and embellishments back from the knitting needle until you wish to wrap them around the knitting needle.

4. Push the seed beads and any dangles down the wire next to the knitting needle, and wrap the beaded wire around the needle until the bead reaches the desired size. See inset photo at bottom right.

Book Accented with Dyed Cheese-cloth, a Metal Embellishment, and a Cardstock Motif

The painted cover of this cardstock book is given textural interest by gluing a piece of dyed cheesecloth to the front. A cardstock motif accents the center and a decorated piece of metal is attached over the dyed cheesecloth. A painted band of paper is used to keep the book closed. It is accented with a piece of air-dry clay and a few pieces of yarn for dimensional interest.

5. Wrap the wire around the needle again for the same distance as at the beginning of the bead.

6. Trim the wire from the spool, 2" from the bead.

7. Remove the bead from the needle. Slip the end of the wire up through the bead, making a small loop on the opposite end.

8. Snip off any excess wire that protrudes from the end of the bead.

More Ideas

These wire beads show some possibilities using various wire colors, charms, and multiple groups of beads.

Embossed Metal Embellishments

1. Cut a piece of fine-gauge metal to the desired size and adhere to a piece of adhesive fun foam.
2. Use a ballpoint pen or metal embossing tool to draw a design onto the thin metal sheet (top right).
3. Use Sharpie markers to apply color to the metal sheet (center right).
4. Cut out the design, and color the edges of the foam with a Sharpie marker (bottom right).

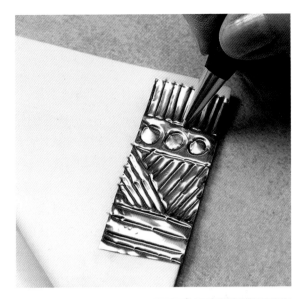

More Ideas

These metal embellishments demonstrate how embossing the metal with various designs and using different marker colors can create a variety of accents.

METAL GALLERY

Freestanding Plastic Frame with a Doll and Metal Embellishments

For this design, the inside back and outside edges of an 8" x 10" plastic shadowbox frame were stamped using Jacquard's Piñata Colors. Additional Piñata Color was sponged on the right and left of the stamped design on the inside back of the frame. After the color was dry, the same design was rubber-stamped over the first pattern using Sherrill's Sorbets in Mint. Angelina, embossed fun foam, painted wooden squares, and metal grids were glued to the collage surface. A thin metal embossed piece was added to the right side of the design just below the center and a stuffed doll accent was glued to the left of the design. For the base, a 1" x 4" board about 14" long was painted with Violet Neopaque, and designs were stamped along the top. The framed collage was attached to the painted board with Crafter's Pick The Ultimate! adhesive.

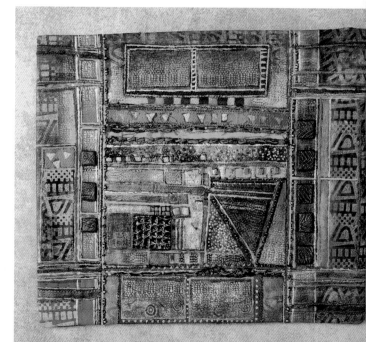

Stamped Collage with Accents of Fun Foam, Pipe Cleaners, and Metal Shapes

An 8" x 10" piece of cardboard was painted and then stamped with a variety of patterns to create the background of this collage. A piece of painted and stamped black fabric accents the right side of the design. A piece of fun foam decorated with a repeat Styrofoam print pattern is glued to the left of the design, extending beyond the edge. Two wrapped chenille pipe cleaners are glued to the surface of the fun foam. A piece of rubber-stamped metal mesh is glued between the wrapped pipe cleaners. A heated and rubber-stamped piece of Styrofoam was slipped onto a pipe cleaner and then the pipe cleaner was wrapped with textured yarn and attached just to the right of the center of the cardboard background. Two metal triangles are glued to the right of the pipe cleaner. A rubber-stamped piece of fun foam is glued to the right of the design with the edges extended.

Small Wall Hanging with Beads, Air-Dry Clay, and a Metal Embellishment

This small painted wall hanging has been given a dimensional surface with the addition of lines and dots made with applicator-tipped paint. Decorative yarn, seed beads, and small gold square beads are also stitched to the surface for dimension. Eight air-dry clay embellishments are attached to the wall hanging and a piece of thin embossed metal is glued to the lower left to complete the design.

LAMINATED ACCENTS

Laminated jewelry and dangles make wonderful embellishments. I use a Xyron machine for my laminating; it places laminate over the front and back of the piece, making it easy to crop the design close to the edges. Because Xyron machines don't use electricity, they are easy to bring to classes or on vacation. Electric laminators laminate only the area not covered by the design, so they are wonderful for adding ribbons and yarn on top of the design. Laminating machines are available at many craft stores. Some craft, rubber-stamping, and scrapbooking stores also have Xyron machines available for customers to use.

Using a Xyron Machine to Make Laminated Accents

1. Make a series of rubber-stamped or painted designs on cardstock or heavy paper.
2. Paint the back of the paper with designs and coordinating colors of your choice.
3. Feed the painted paper into the Xyron machine, following the manufacturer's directions. The front side of the design should be placed face up through the laminator.

Xyron Laminated Fish Necklace

Laminated fish designs dangle from a crocheted necklace cord. The dangles are attached to the crocheted chain with decorative threads and cords, which were left long for a textural effect. The crocheted chain was decorated further with bead embellishments. The backs of the dangles were painted with Jacquard's Piñata Colors, which work well on nonporous surfaces.

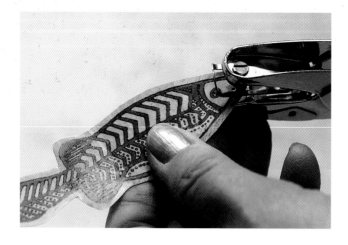

4. After you finish laminating, cut the designs apart to use for embellishments (above).

5. Punch holes in the laminated pieces using a ¹⁄₁₆" hole punch if desired (left).

More Ideas

These pieces show some of the possibilities for creating laminated accents from stamped and painted designs.

LAMINATE GALLERY

Book with Air-Dry Clay Piece and Electrically Laminated Dangles

This stamped book, made from stapled cardstock, uses a horizontal cardstock band as a closure. The band is embellished by punching holes in it near the center and sewing on dangles that were laminated with an electric machine. The sewing-thread ends are allowed to hang from the band for added interest. A painted air-dry clay piece is glued over the holes.

Two Laminated Pins

These two pins were made with an electric laminator. Lay out the materials for the pins, starting with fabric as well as painted cardstock. Add ribbons, cords, and metallic cords over the fabric and paper. Laminate the collaged materials, and then cut them out in free-form shapes. Give a finished look to the pieces by adding paint to the edges of the designs.

Laminated Petroglyph Necklace

Stamped petroglyph images are laminated and attached to a crocheted chain of multicolored yarns. The images are attached to the chain with decorative threads that are allowed to dangle for textural interest. Gold square beads are stitched along the length of the crocheted necklace chain to add sparkle. Star charms and other metal dangles also add interest along the chain.

Puzzle-Piece Necklace with Laminated Dangles

A large puzzle piece was covered with a molding-paste impressed design. Then Lumiere paint was painted over the dried molding-paste design. A painted air-dry clay piece is attached to the puzzle piece to add depth and texture. A 1/16" punch was used to make holes along the bottom edge of the puzzle piece so that laminated dangles could be attached with decorative threads. The thread ends hang freely from the necklace, creating a wispy fringe. Additional holes punched in the top of the puzzle piece are used for attaching it to a crocheted chain with small strands of seed beads. An air-dry clay button and a buttonhole are used at the ends of the crocheted chain to make the closure.

Bracelet with Laminated Dangles

This simple, yet elaborate-looking bracelet is made by covering a thick elastic band that will stretch easily over the wrist with painted 1/2" fabric strips and stitching them in place. To make sure the bracelet isn't constricting, pull the band while wrapping with the fabric to stretch it out a bit. Several laminated dangles of similar shape and size were created, and each was attached to the bracelet band with a length of four seed beads. The dangles were stitched 1/8" apart around the entire band to create this effect. Note that you should not use hair bands precovered with fabric for this project; they will pucker and will be too thick when wrapping with fabric.

TYVEK EMBELLISHMENTS

I think that Tyvek has magical properties when used for embellishments. Many artists have experimented with its possibilities. Tyvek has been used for insulating buildings, for strong mailing envelopes, for decorative clothing, and for disposable clothing used in industry. When heated, Tyvek shrinks up, creating a strong, unbreakable piece that is very lightweight. Heating Tyvek with a heat gun can cause some noxious fumes, so I have been experimenting with a safe way to heat it without health issues arising. Tyvek can be toxic if air reaches it when heating, so be sure to heat Tyvek between Teflon ironing sheets in a well-ventilated area.

Ironed Tyvek Embellishments

1. Cut a square or rectangle of Tyvek. Lay the Tyvek on your work surface and paint light layers of color over the entire surface. Let the paint dry and then place the Tyvek on a Teflon ironing sheet.
2. Cover the Tyvek with a second Teflon ironing sheet. Set the iron on the polyester setting and let it heat to that temperature.
3. Gently iron the Tyvek between the Teflon sheets, checking it frequently to monitor the amount of shrinkage. Ironing too much will cause holes in the design (which can also add interest to your piece). If the Tyvek isn't shrinking, set the iron a little hotter and let it reach that temperature. Check the Tyvek frequently to see if shrinking has begun, and stop when you are happy with the results. One side of the Tyvek will have a raised design similar to reptile skin; the other side will have a recessed design. See inset photo below, which shows the recessed design.

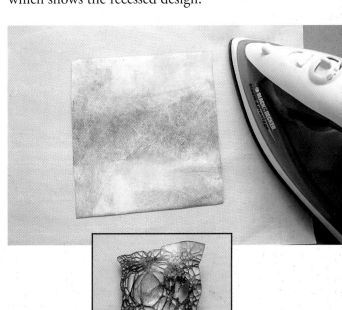

Small Inkjet Wall Hanging with Tyvek Embellishments

The background of this piece was printed on an inkjet printer and enhanced with paint. It is accented just above the center with six painted and ironed Tyvek pieces. Two longer Tyvek pieces are overlapped and glued to the piece near the bottom edge. An ironed metallic gold Styrofoam piece accents the top edge. Lines of applicator-tipped paint are added for more dimensional interest.

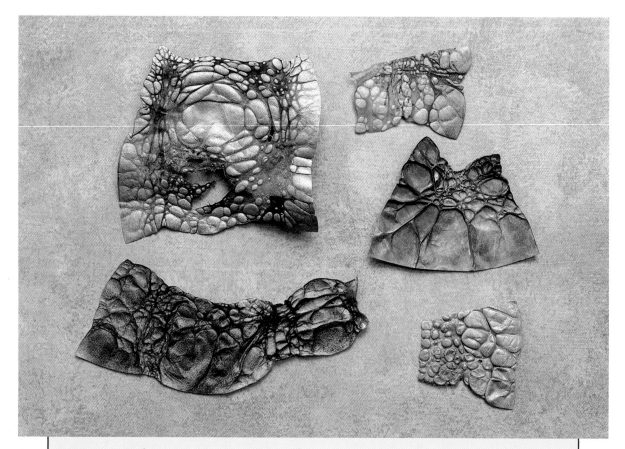

More Ideas

These pieces show some of the many outcomes that can result when ironing Tyvek.

Deep-Embossed Tyvek Embellishments

1. Follow step 1 of "Ironed Tyvek Embellishments" on page 61.
2. Lay a rubber stamp under the Tyvek. Cover the Tyvek with a second Teflon ironing sheet. Set the iron on the polyester setting and let it heat to that temperature.
3. Follow step 3 of "Ironed Tyvek Embellishments." The finished piece will have a slightly raised design that mimics the rubber-stamped image. Sometimes the iron can be too hot to achieve the desired effect, so iron very gently and for only a few seconds.

Making a Thick, Embossed Tyvek Embellishment

1. Place a rubber stamp on a Teflon ironing sheet.
2. Cut five to nine small Tyvek squares or rectangles. Layer them to make a stack, and place the stack on top of the rubber stamp. Lay another Teflon ironing sheet on top of the Tyvek pieces. Iron at the hottest setting, keeping the iron in place until the Tyvek has melted.
3. Remove the stamp, replace the Teflon sheet, and iron the layers of Tyvek together around the edges. Remove the Teflon ironing sheet.
4. Paint the Tyvek using sponge painting or a dry brush, building layers of color gradually.
5. Trim the design to size, if desired.

More Ideas

These examples illustrate what happens when ironing a stack of Tyvek pieces over deep-etched rubber stamps.

TYVEK GALLERY

Wall Hanging with Tyvek and Abalone Shells

This piece was made as a demonstration at Rainbow Silks for a class about wall hangings. The background was sponged, painted, and layered with rubber-stamping. Appliqué pieces were glued in place, and cording and beads were sewn on to further adorn the surface. Six painted Tyvek pieces accent the wall hanging, and three abalone shell pieces, glued close to each other, create a focal point.

Wall Hanging with Wrapped Pipe Cleaners and Tyvek Embellishments

A painted wall hanging is sectioned off with six wrapped pipe-cleaner embellishments. Four Tyvek embellishments, each created by ironing a stack of Tyvek pieces, are glued to the wall hanging. Applicator-tipped paint lines further accent the piece.

Sewn Tyvek Embellishment

An 8" x 10" piece of Tyvek was painted with Neopaque and Lumiere paints and then ironed to create this large embellishment. The finished piece was machine stitched to a piece of painted fabric. After stitching, more paint and sewing were added for a layered effect. Selected areas of the design were also accented with lines and dots made with applicator-tipped paint.

Tyvek Necklace

A painted and stuffed fabric triangle is accented with a large painted and ironed Tyvek embellishment, as well as a second Tyvek embellishment that was formed by fusing several layers of painted Tyvek together. A shrink-plastic button, textured cording, and beads also decorate the piece. Applicator-tipped paint was added to the design to highlight selected areas. The finished piece is attached to a folded fabric band to complete the necklace. Beads accent the fabric band and a fabric loop and button are used for the closure.

SHRINK-PLASTIC ACCENTS

Shrink plastic has been available for many years and offers wonderful opportunities for embellishing projects and making jewelry. It comes in several colors and can be rubber-stamped with stamp-pad ink for nonporous surfaces, or painted and stamped with Jacquard's Piñata Colors after the plastic has shrunk. Finished pieces can also be colored with Sharpie markers or nail polish. Shrink plastic can be used to make buttons, beads, dangles, and other embellishments.

Flat Shrink-Plastic Buttons, Pins, or Dangles

1. Cut out a piece of shrink plastic. Apply rubber-stamp designs using stamp pad ink for nonporous surfaces. I used Jacquard's Pearl Ex stamp pads for this project.
2. For buttons, punch two holes in the shrink plastic. For dangles, punch one hole with a ⅛" hole punch.
3. Lay the shrink plastic on a glazed ceramic tile.
4. Hold the shrink-plastic piece in place on the tile with a metal knitting needle. Use a pot holder to hold the needle. Heat the shrink plastic with a heat gun such as Ranger's Heat it Craft Tool until the plastic warps, thickens, and flattens.

Wall Hanging with Pipe-Cleaner and Shrink-Plastic Embellishments

Rubber-stamped images cover the background of this painted wall hanging. A wrapped pipe-cleaner embellishment is secured just to the right of the center of the design and four shrink-plastic accents align in a vertical column on the right side. Applicator-tipped paint adds subtle dimension to selected areas.

5. Press another glazed ceramic tile on the shrink plastic to flatten it until it cools.
6. Remove the tile to reveal the finished design.

More Ideas

These shrink-plastic pieces show some of the color and design options for making buttons and dangles.

Shrink-Plastic Beads

1. Cut a strip of shrink plastic in the color of your choice. Round the corners of the strip with scissors.
2. Color the shrink plastic with rubber-stamped designs. Use a stamp-pad ink for nonporous surfaces. Allow to dry overnight or gently heat with a heat gun to dry the ink.
3. Roll up the strip of decorated shrink plastic on a knitting needle with the design side out, securing it in place with a small rubber band. Put the rolled up piece on a metal knitting needle. Hold the end of

the knitting needle with a pot holder. Lay the knitting needle's end on the top of a ceramic tile.

4. Heat the shrink plastic with a heat gun. After the shrink plastic has fused together, remove the rubber band. Continue to apply heat until the bead shrinks completely.

5. Take a large unmounted rubber stamp and wrap it around the heated bead to remove the bead from the knitting needle. If you press hard on the rubber stamp, it will add a nice texture to the bead.

CREATING FAUX-GLASS BEADS

Clear shrink plastic looks like glass when colored with transparent inks or markers. It is sometimes hard to control the result, but the pieces you get are unusual and wonderful for embellishments or jewelry. It is one of the harder shrink plastics to use for beads because clear shrink plastic doesn't easily adhere to itself, but the results are well worth the effort.

More Ideas
These pieces include transparent beads and opaque beads made from shrink plastic.

Dimensional Shrink-Plastic Accents

1. Lay two or three pieces of shrink plastic, cut in graduated sizes, on top of a Teflon ironing sheet (top left).
2. Lay another Teflon ironing sheet on top of the shrink plastic.
3. With a hot iron set on a dry setting, iron the plastic until it shrinks, waves, and then flattens. Peek under the Teflon sheet to see when it is ready.
4. Remove the top Teflon sheet. Immediately press a rubber stamp into the hot plastic to create a dimensional design (center left).
5. Trim any jagged edges with sharp scissors.
6. Color the shrink-plastic piece with Piñata Colors, nail polish, or Sharpie markers.
7. Add Lumiere metallic color to the edges by brush, sponge, or with your fingers.

Shrink-Plastic Pin Accented with a Fabric Bead (left)

This collage-style pin was created by first making a shrink-plastic piece and then texturing it with layers of acrylic paint. Seed beads were glued to the surface of the shrink plastic and selected areas were highlighted with applicator-tipped paint. A wrapped fabric bead, embellished with seed beads, serves as the focal point. A pin was glued to the back side.

More Ideas

These pieces show the variety that is possible when layering and ironing shrink plastic, and then pressing a rubber stamp into the hot surface.

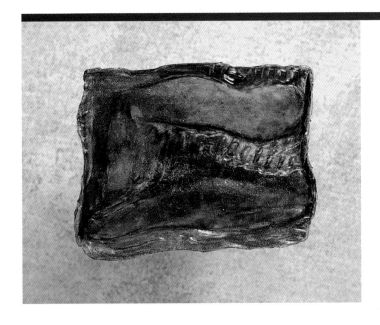

Two Ironed Shrink-Plastic Pins

Ironed layers of clear shrink plastic produced these textured pieces. They were colored with Jacquard's Piñata Colors and metallic markers. Pin backs were glued to the backs of the pieces.

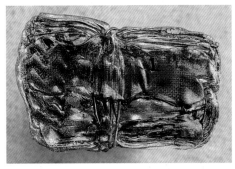

SHRINK-PLASTIC GALLERY

Three Shrink-Plastic Pins

These shrink-plastic pieces feature painted and stamped designs. The top pin is embellished with wire wrapping and a Chinese coin. The other two pins are made by gluing a small shrink-plastic embellishment over a larger piece. Pin backs are glued to the designs to allow wearability.

Necklace with Shrink-Plastic Beads and Knotted Beads

Several beads made from knotted fabric alternate with shrink-plastic beads on a flexible gold plastic cord. Commercial beads are added on both sides to finish the necklace.

Shrink-Plastic Necklace with Odd-Shaped Beads

Translucent shrink plastic was used to make eight beads for this necklace. The beads are painted with various shades of green and gold Neopaque and strung on a plastic cord with metal discs in between. Metal beads added at the ends of the cord finish off the necklace.

Card with Shrink-Plastic Button

A piece of black cardstock was enhanced with Rollagraph images and sponged paint. The edge was cut into a wavy pattern and then a second narrow, wavy strip was cut from the edge. The patterned cardstock and patterned wavy strip were then glued a short distance apart to a piece of green cardstock that was folded in half to make a card. The right edge of the green cardstock was cut in a wavy pattern. A shrink-plastic button was sewn to the front of the card with metallic thread strung with small copper beads. The ends of the thread hang from the shrink-plastic button for textural interest.

SHEET-PROTECTOR EMBELLISHMENTS

I discovered the process for making sheet-protector embellishments by accident. I was teaching a class and had a "What if?" moment. I found that ironing plastic sheet protectors with collage bits sandwiched between them yielded wonderful results. I know you'll have fun with this process.

Creating Sheet-Protector Embellishments

1. Cut a square from a plastic sheet protector, being sure that a fold from the sheet protector remains along one edge.
2. Place pieces of painted fabric or thin paper, cords, textured yarn, or any other flat embellishment next to the fold. Trim most of the embellishments so that the plastic sheet protector extends about ½" beyond the colored pieces (top right).
3. Place the piece between two Teflon ironing sheets and iron on a polyester setting. Do not overheat or the plastic will bubble. Keep checking every few seconds (center right).
4. Press a ceramic tile over the Teflon, covering the design, to flatten after ironing. Remove the tile and Teflon sheet.
5. Add color to the piece with Sharpie markers and trim to the desired shape (bottom right).

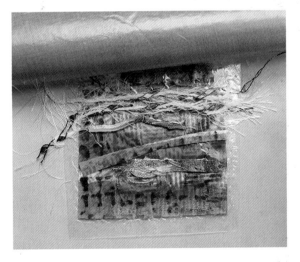

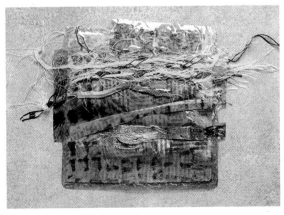

Stapled Book with a Large Sheet-Protector Embellishment

A variety of rubber stamps and metallic paints were used to decorate the cover of a stapled book. A large sheet-protector embellishment with a bead accent creates a focal point on the cover.

More Ideas

Working with sheet protectors offers many striking possibilities, as shown in these examples.

Textured Sheet-Protector Beads

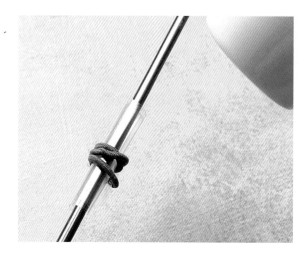

1. Cut a strip from a plastic sheet protector.
2. Wrap the strip around a metal knitting needle and secure it in place with an elastic band.
3. Hold onto the end of the knitting needle with a lightweight pot holder. Heat the rolled sheet protector with a heat gun until it starts to adhere to itself.
4. Turn off the heat gun and remove the elastic band. Continue to heat the plastic until it has melted.
5. Wrap an unmounted, textured rubber stamp around the bead and press to make an impression; use the stamp to slide the hot bead off the knitting needle. If you'd like to keep the bead smooth, use the smooth side of the stamp to slide the bead off the knitting needle. To make a scrunched bead, use the rubber stamp to pull the bead off the needle while it's still hot and scrunch the plastic together for a wrinkled effect.
6. Color the bead with Sharpie markers.
7. Embellish the bead with paint, yarn, seed beads, or other accents of your choice. You can also insert a few short fibers into the rolled-up sheet protector before heating for a different effect.

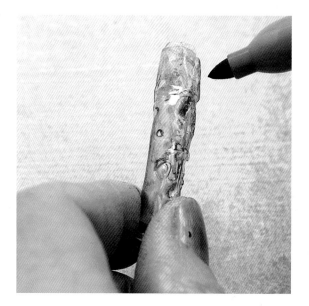

More Ideas

These samples show sheet-protector beads with threads, yarn, and wire prestrung with beads. At right is a scrunched bead colored with markers.

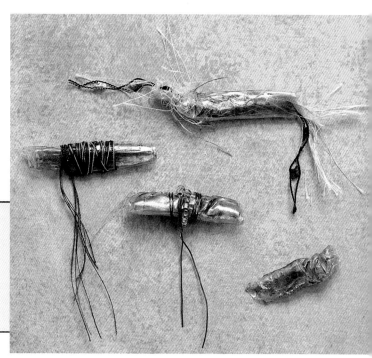

SHEET-PROTECTOR GALLERY

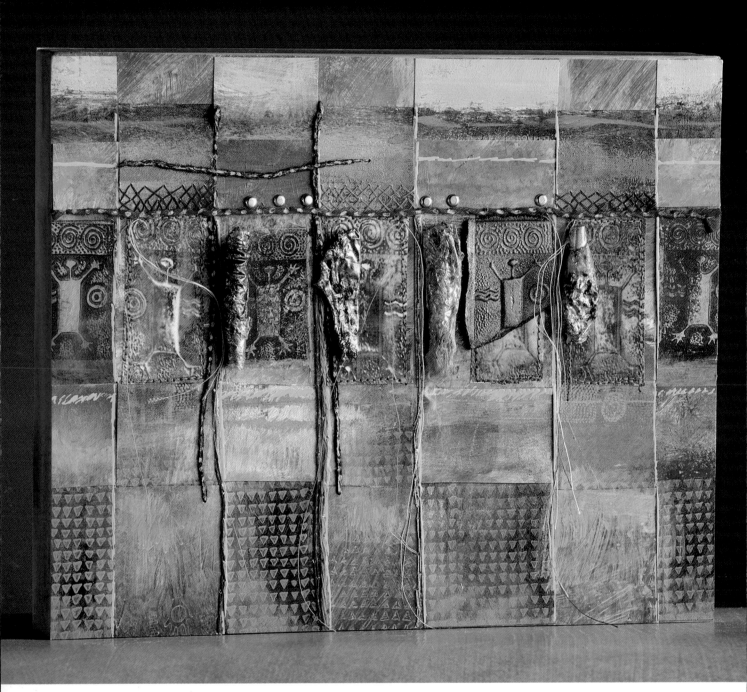

Woven Paper Design with Sheet-Protector Beads

A woven design made from painted cardstock is given added dimension with machine stitching and hand stitching. Inkjet collage pieces were glued over some of the woven areas, along with four sheet-protector beads. The entire design was mounted onto a piece of cardboard that was glued to the cardboard insert from a plastic frame. The cardboard insert was painted along the edges to coordinate with the design. An additional 8" x 10" piece of mat board was glued to the back of the piece and a sawtooth hanger was glued to the mat board on the back of the finished design.

Necklace with Large Fabric Bead

A colorful sheet-protector piece is used as the base for a necklace. It is decorated with Jacquard's Piñata Colors, which are transparent. A large embellished fabric bead is glued to the surface with Crafter's Pick The Ultimate! adhesive. The entire piece is attached to an elastic band with thread accented with seed beads.

Cheesecloth Pin with Large Sheet-Protector Bead

A painted piece of cheesecloth was manipulated into a pleasing shape, and then it was stitched with a needle and matching thread to hold that shape. Painted fabric strips were sewn over the piece and a large sheet-protector bead was sewn on top. Seed-bead embellishments, a wire bead, and a shrink-plastic dangle complete the collage. A pin back was sewn to the back of the design.

Necklace with Tyvek Beads, Fabric Beads, and a Large Sheet-Protector Bead

A variety of beads were created and strung onto black plastic cord to make this necklace. A sheet-protector bead accents the center. A painted fabric bead is attached to each end of the cord.

FUN-FOAM EMBELLISHMENTS

Fun foam is a product that is sold in many forms in craft stores. It is usually found in the children's section and comes in sheets of different sizes and thicknesses. There are adhesive-backed pieces that can be cut in any shape and attached to your projects. Large pieces can be painted, cut into any shape, and then heated and molded. You can press deep-etched rubber stamps into fun foam to make impressions that can be painted and embellished. You can make buttons and beads and pins. You can make necklaces or use fun foam as a backing for other materials. It is strong and resilient and comes in many colors and thicknesses. You can punch holes in it, sew it (with some sewing machines), stitch beads to it, or manipulate it in any way you wish. I think you'll love working with this product.

Creating Fun-Foam Embellishments

1. Cut or tear the fun foam into the desired shape.
2. Using a heat gun, heat the fun foam on a heat-resistant surface such as a ceramic tile. A knitting needle can help you hold the foam in place during heating.

Small Wall Hanging with Machine-Sewn Collage and a Chenille Pipe-Cleaner Embellishment

Painted fabric was used to make a small wall hanging. Additional painted strips were appliquéd with a sewing machine to add decoration to the surface. Matching painted fabric strips were used to create a wrapped pipe-cleaner embellishment. A fun foam embellishment, highlighted with applicator-tipped paint, becomes a focal point.

3. While the fun foam is hot, press a deep-etched rubber stamp firmly into the surface.

4. After the fun foam has cooled, paint it with layers of dry-brushed color (see "Dry Brushing" on page 17). Add details with a detail brush.

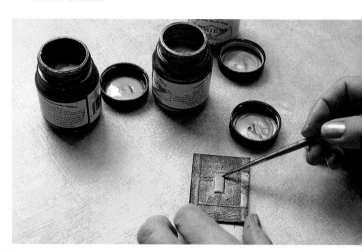

More Ideas

Here are some eye-catching samples of stamp-impressed fun foam in different shapes.

Fun-Foam Pendants

1. Repeat steps 1 and 2 of "Creating Fun-Foam Embellishments" on page 81.

2. While the foam is hot, roll the edge over a knitting needle and keep heating it until the foam attaches to the base piece for a pendant.

3. Leave the knitting needle in place, and press a rubber stamp into the edge of the hot fun foam. Let cool.

4. After the fun foam has cooled, remove it from the knitting needle and paint it with layers of dry-brushed color (see "Dry Brushing" on page 17).

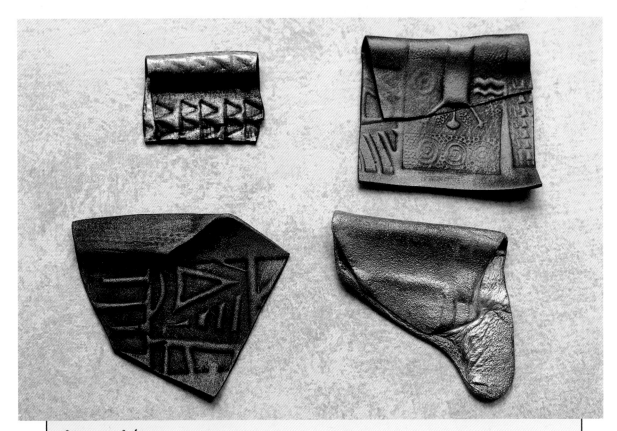

More Ideas
There are many possible pendant shapes, as shown in this photo.

Fun-Foam Beads

1. Roll a strip of fun foam around a knitting needle and place, seam side down, on a heat-resistant surface such as a ceramic tile.
2. Heat the fun foam until it attaches to itself.
3. Wrap a rubber stamp around the hot fun foam while it is still on the needle and impress the design into the foam.
4. Remove the stamp. When the foam bead has cooled, remove it from the knitting needle and paint it with dry-brushed layers of paint (see "Dry Brushing" on page 17).

More Ideas
When making beads with fun foam, you can shape and paint your beads in a variety of ways.

Fun-Foam Buttons

1. Follow steps 1–3 of "Creating Fun-Foam Embellishments" on pages 81–82. If desired, fold over one edge of the foam before making the impression.
2. Paint the foam piece with dry-brushed layers of paint (see "Dry Brushing" on page 17).
3. Punch two or more holes in the foam with a ¹⁄₁₆" hole punch.
4. Add more paint to the button, if desired.

FUN-FOAM TIPS

- **Making double-layer buttons.** You can use two layers of fun foam for stronger buttons and each can be a slightly different size for more interest.
- **Buttons embellished with seed beads.** Sew the button to the desired surface, stitching seed beads into the open spaces.
- **Using fun foam with an adhesive surface as a stabilizer for embellishments.** Decorated surfaces such as fabric, metal sheet, or paper can be stabilized by using fun foam as a backing. Small collages can also be mounted on fun foam for stability. Apply the embellishments to the backing and cut to size. Or, for collages, cut the fun foam ⅛" from the edge of the collage and decorate the edge with painted lines or create dots with applicator-tipped paint.
- **Using fun foam as a surface for painting and rubber-stamping.** I was teaching a collage class when one of my students, Suzi Brown, started collaging and painting on fun foam. It hadn't occurred to me to paint on fun foam, but it is really an excellent surface and doesn't seem to buckle. Using any of the painting and rubber-stamping techniques described on pages 17–23, simply paint and rubber-stamp on fun foam in the colors of your choice.

More Ideas
You can make unique fun-foam buttons in an assortment of shapes, sizes, and colors as shown here.

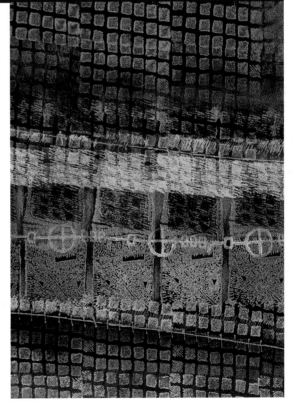

This colorful piece was created by layering stamped, sponged, and dry-sponged color on black fun foam. Selected areas were highlighted with applicator-tipped paint.

FUN-FOAM GALLERY

Violet Book with Fun-Foam Embellishment

Rubber-stamped and painted designs decorate the front cover of this stapled book. A stamped and painted fun-foam embellishment is glued to the center of the book cover, over a few strands of textured yarn.

Fun-Foam Pins

These pins were created by stenciling designs onto white cotton fabric and decorating them with more paint, applicator-tipped highlights, and permanent-marker highlights. The designs were then mounted on black fun foam and trimmed ⅛" from the edges, leaving a narrow black border around each. More detail was added to the designs and the borders with a small brush and Lumiere paint. Pin backs were glued to the back of the shapes to turn them into jewelry.

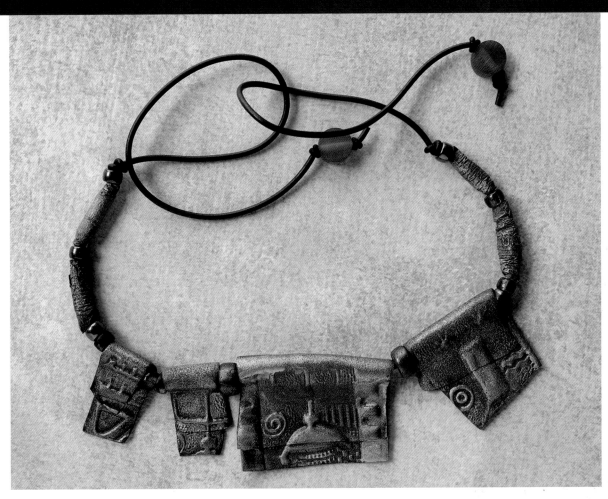

Fun-Foam Necklace

Fun-foam pendant pieces were strung onto a piece of plastic cord along with a few painted paper beads and commercial beads. Resin beads were added at the end of the cord for a nice finishing effect.

Fun-Foam Pin

An irregular piece of black fun foam was heated and folded onto itself to create this unique shape. The right edge of the piece was allowed to curl during the heating process. The piece was rubber-stamped with a design and then painted with dry-brushing techniques. A pin back was glued to the back of the piece.

PAPER AND FABRIC MOTIFS

Fabric and cardstock motifs are among my favorite embellishments. They are easy to create, very strong, and add wonderful texture and color to any project. You can decorate the fabric or paper using any paint or color application of your choice. Rubber-stamped images work especially well.

Creating Paper and Fabric Motifs

1. Decorate cardstock or fabric with paint, rubber-stamping, glazing, or other methods of your choice. The sample shown here is fabric.
2. Squeeze a generous line of Crafter's Pick The Ultimate! adhesive onto the back of the decorated piece.
3. Use a scraper or old credit card to spread the glue across the back of the decorated surface. There should be a layer of glue about 1/16" thick. If the glue is spread too thin it won't adhere to the surface. Apply more glue as needed.
4. Glue the fabric to a plain piece of fabric and press the two pieces firmly in place by hand.

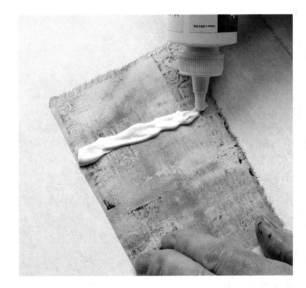

Fabric Motif Necklace

A variety of fabric motifs were made from rubber-stamp images of dolls and abstract shapes. The pieces were sewn with metallic thread to a piece of cord made from painted fabric, and the thread tails were allowed to hang down over the motifs. This necklace was created during a demonstration at Rainbow Silks in England

5. Glue the piece to another piece of decorated or plain fabric. If the back of the piece will be seen, be sure to use decorated fabric for this step. If you are gluing the piece to decorated fabric, place the fabric decorated side down. Trim off the excess paper or fabric.

6. Let the glue dry.

7. Trim the design as needed. If there is a complex design like an animal or fish, use sharp scissors to cut out the motif.

USING IRON-ON ADHESIVE

Instead of glue, the layers of fabric or paper can be adhered together with layers of iron-on adhesive, such as Wonder Under.

More Ideas
Use your imaginaton to create fabric motifs in a range of shapes and sizes.

Cardstock Book with Inner and Outer Covers and Various Embellishments

Rubber-stamped layers of paint were used to decorate the cover of a simple cardstock book. Several fabric motifs were created and glued to the surface, including a Dye-na-Flow-colored doll and a triangle embellished with seed beads. Additional paint stripes were applied to selected areas and an embossed and colored piece of metal was glued to the right side of the cover as a finishing touch.

Fabric Motif Bracelet

A rubber-stamp design was used to make seven fabric motifs. Sherrill's Sorbets and a detail brush were used to accent the stamped designs. The motifs were then glued to bracelet links, available at jewelry-supply stores. The bracelet is finished off by connecting a large jump ring to one end and a metal clasp to the other end.

Fabric Motif Glued to a Decorated CD Case

For this piece, a thin CD case was decorated on the inside and outside with Pearl Ex stamp-pad inks. The inks were allowed to dry and then lightly heat set with a Ranger Heat it Craft Tool. Don't overheat or the CD case will warp. Move the craft tool over the whole piece in a circular motion to avoid burning the plastic. A painted piece of cardstock was cut to size and inserted into the CD case. A strip of cardstock the same size as the top of the CD case was painted and then glued in place. A painted fabric motif was glued to the finished CD case with Crafter's Pick The Ultimate! adhesive.

Painted and Rubber-Stamped Vest with Fabric Motifs

This vest was made using my own pattern and fabric that had been painted and rubber-stamped. Fabric motifs and lines of seed beads are attached to the vest to give it some dimensional interest.

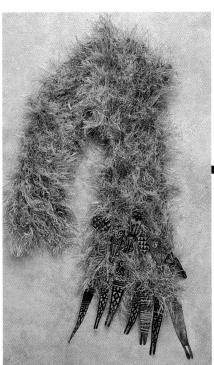

Padded Necklace with Fabric Motifs

A textured stuffed shape is used as the base for this necklace. A piece of heated and painted Styrofoam was glued across the top. Three Peruvian figures were stamped next to each other, embellished with paint, and turned into a fabric motif. The unit was cut out as one large fabric motif. Fabric cord was threaded through a hole punched in the motif and knotted, and then the fabric motif was glued to the Styrofoam piece so the fabric cord was centered. A Tyvek bead was glued to the upper-right corner of the necklace for interest.

Knitted Yarn and Fabric Motif Scarf

A simple rectangular scarf was knitted with Fun Fur from Lyon Brand yarns. Fabric motifs were hand sewn in a staggered pattern on the bottom of the scarf.

WRAPPED CHENILLE PIPE CLEANERS

I learned about wrapping chenille pipe cleaners with fabric, yarn, and cord from an article by Maggie Grey in her Workshop on the Web. Since I began wrapping pipe cleaners, I have discovered endless possibilities for creating with them. Once decorated, the pipe cleaners are easily attached to a variety of projects with glue or stitching. Chenille pipe cleaners are found in craft stores and are available in various colors and sizes.

Creating Wrapped Chenille Pipe Cleaners

1. Cut a pipe cleaner to the desired length with sharp scissors. Choose yarn, cord, or a fabric strip or strips in colors that will coordinate with your project.
2. Lay the end of a piece of yarn, cord, or fabric strip over the end of the pipe cleaner for about 1".
3. Start wrapping over the pipe cleaner, overlapping the end where the yarn, cord, or fabric strip began.
4. To create a bead effect, wrap over and over in the same spot, building up layers. Repeat as desired.
5. When you get to the end of the pipe cleaner, cut off the excess yarn, cord, or fabric strip, leaving about ½".

Cardstock Collage Embellished with Wrapped Chenille Pipe Cleaners and a Fabric Motif

Painted and rubber-stamped paper and fabric pieces were glued and machine sewn onto cardstock to create a collage background. Applicator-tipped paint was used to highlight selected areas. Two wrapped chenille pipe cleaners and a fabric motif add further decoration to the surface.

6. Apply glue to the cut end of the yarn, cord, or fabric strip, and wrap it back onto the pipe cleaner, rolling the pipe cleaner as you go.

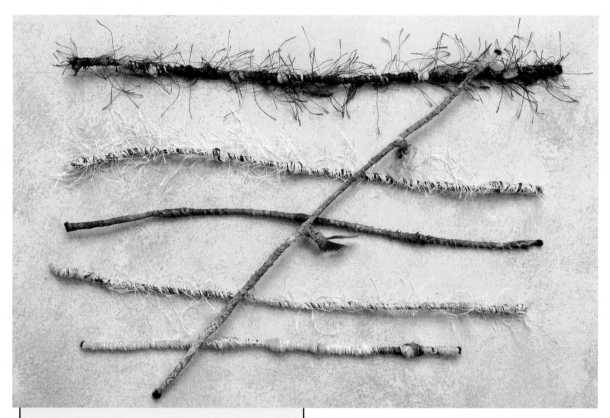

More Ideas

These dazzling pieces are just a few samples of what you can achieve when you wrap chenille pipe cleaners with fabric strips, decorative threads, or yarn.

Pipe Cleaner Necklace with Fabric Beads

To create the base for this necklace, two chenille pipe cleaners were overlapped for about 3", twisted together, and then wrapped with decorative threads. Eight fabric-covered and yarn-embellished drinking-straw beads were threaded onto the wrapped chenille necklace. To wear the necklace, the two ends are twisted together at the back of the neck.

WRAPPED CHENILLE PIPE CLEANERS GALLERY

Painted and Collaged Tile

This project began with an unglazed ceramic tile. The tile was textured with molding paste, and then painted fabric and paper were collaged to the surface. The dried molding paste was painted and then additional paint and applicator-tipped lines were applied until the desired result was achieved. The surface is embellished with two air-dry clay pieces, three commercial buttons, and a wrapped chenille pipe cleaner.

Cardstock Book

The black cardstock cover for this book was embellished using cardboard and rubber-band prints, rubber-stamping, and Rollagraph lines. The cover is folded so that about 2" of the inner back cover shows, offering an extra opportunity for stamping and Rollagraph designs. A chenille pipe-cleaner embellishment is decorated with a painted Style Stone from Clearsnap, wrapped with decorative thread, and secured to the inside back cover of the book.

Bracelet with Style Stones

Two Style Stones of painted fish and a heart Style Stone were threaded onto a chenille pipe cleaner. The ends of the pipe cleaner were wrapped around each other to form the bracelet and then the pipe cleaner was wrapped with decorative yarn.

STENCILING TECHNIQUES

Stenciling has been an art form for many centuries. Cavemen placed their hands on cave walls and blew color through tubes in the space around their hands to create stenciled designs.

Today, plastic stencils come in many shapes and sizes and are available at most craft stores. A plastic stencil has a cutout in it, which allows paint to be applied through the opening. Any flat item with an opening cut into it can be used as a stencil. Creating simple stencil shapes using stencil plastic is easy. This section will explore a variety of creative techniques using stencils.

Applying Color through Stencil Openings

1. Place a stencil on the design surface and tape securely in place. If using paper or cardstock, use paper tape.
2. Apply color through the stencil openings using one of the following four methods:

Sponging. Apply paint or stamp-pad ink to a sponge square. Pat off excess paint. Pat the color through the stencil opening. Work from light to dark. Reapply color as needed.

Stippling. Add the color through the stencil opening with a stencil brush and an up-and-down motion to create texture.

Small Wall Hanging with Stenciled Background

Stenciled fabric was used to create this small wall hanging. Five air-dry clay embellishments add texture to the design.

Rubber-stamping. Apply paint or stamp-pad ink to a rubber stamp. Rubber-stamp an image or images through the stencil opening. Sponge color lightly over the stamped design if desired.

Applying Color with Clearsnap's Style Stones Inking Brush. Apply paint or stamp-pad ink to the inking brush. Apply the paint through the stencil opening using a stippling technique. Note that Clearsnap's inking brush is ideal for going through tiny openings, especially brass stencils.

Outlining the Stencil Opening with Permanent Markers

1. Place a stencil on the design surface and tape securely in place.
2. Outline the inside of the stencil with a permanent marker.

3. Sponge, stipple, rubber-stamp, or use markers through the stencil openings if desired. Remove the stencil.

Drawing into Stencil Openings with Water-Soluble Markers

1. Place a small stencil on a piece of cardstock.
2. Draw lines through the openings with water-soluble markers. Remove the stencil.

3. Spray a light mist of water over the marker lines.
4. Allow the wet marker lines to dry.

Applying Color through Sequin Waste

Sequin waste is available in various sizes. It is a floral supply product and can be purchased at floral supply stores.

1. Lay the sequin waste on the design surface.
2. Use a rotary toothbrush to apply paint or stamp-pad ink through the openings in the sequin waste.
3. Remove the stencil.

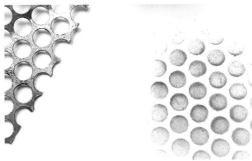

Small Wall Hanging with Stenciled Borders

This design is created by painting a piece of fabric with masking tape resist. Stenciled borders are stitched to each side of the piece. Decorative threads and beads accent the design, along with applicator-tipped paint.

Stenciled and Painted Cardstock Card

The cover of this card was sponged over the entire surface with layers of paint. A toothbrush was used to apply metallic color to part of the surface. A stencil brush was used to apply color through the six large rectangles using Violet Neopaque. Gold lines, applied with an applicator-tipped bottle, outline the sides of the six stenciled squares. Stencil designs from Diane Ericson are added to the background using Sherrill's Sorbets and a stencil brush. A piece of heated metal enhances the card.

Appliquéd and Stenciled Vest

Checkerboards were stenciled over selected areas of this black vest, which was made using my own pattern. Appliqué pieces were sewn over the checkerboard stencil designs. A dry-sponging technique was used over sequin waste to create an uneven circle design over some of the appliqués and the background fabric. Additional appliqués, consisting of painted and stamped fabric, as well as commercial fabric, were added to the vest front and back. More color was added by rubber stamping triangular shapes on the front of the vest. Applicator-tipped lines were used to highlight selected areas.

WEAVING PAPER AND FABRIC

This is a wonderful, simple, and beautiful technique. You can use previously painted paper and fabric to create your woven design. I learned this technique from Anita Dixon, a friend of mine, who is an outstanding weaver. The first piece I made was an absolute joy to create. It was totally different from what I usually do, and I combined a variety of materials into a very small piece. Stiff paper works best, but you can weave lighter-weight papers with care. All fabrics work for this technique, but painted fabric is easier to use, because it is a little stiffer. I think I've just tapped the tip of the iceberg with this technique and look forward to creating many more weavings in the future.

Weaving Techniques

1. Cut a piece of decorated paper or fabric into strips of various widths, cutting in the lengthwise direction and stopping ½" before reaching the end. Cut the strips in straight, wavy, or diagonal lines.
2. From a second piece of decorated paper or fabric, cut one strip at a time all the way across the piece, cutting the strip in the crosswise direction.

Woven Design with Wrapped Chenille Pipe-Cleaner and Tyvek Embellishments

Two pieces of painted cardstock were woven together and sewn in various areas using a machine straight stitch and zigzag stitch. Painted and ironed Tyvek pieces were glued to the design, followed by more machine stitching. Styrofoam pieces, painted gold, were ironed flat and attached to the left side of the design. A wrapped chenille pipe cleaner is glued to the right of the design to create a strong focal point.

3. Weave the strip over and under through the cut strips of the first piece of paper or fabric.

4. Turn the weaving around and push the strip down as far as it will go. Apply glue if necessary to hold the piece in place.

5. Repeat steps 2–4 until the piece is entirely woven.

6. Embellish the design with machine stitching

WEAVING GALLERY

Small Wall Hanging with Tags

This is the first paper weaving I did. The weaving was made from painted watercolor paper and has machine stitching and decorative yarn added to the surface for texture. The piece was sewn by machine to a heavy piece of cardstock. A thin piece of heated and crimped metal and a piece of air-dry clay were added to the surface for embellishment. A painted wooden square was attached to the surface with a thin foam mounting square. The three hanging tags are painted, stamped, and glazed with Jacquard's textile paint. Small decorative wooden toothpicks were used to attach the tags to the work by sewing them with a zigzag stitch. To hang the piece, a painted chopstick, wrapped with coordinating strips of paper around it, was attached to the hanging with painted wooden squares that were glued to both the chopstick and the hanging.

WEAVING GALLERY *continued*

Small Sculpture with Woven Background Mounted to a Shadowbox Frame

This design is contained within an 8" x 10" plastic shadowbox frame. A woven piece was embellished with machine stitching, watercolor pieces, and Angelina pieces. The woven collage was stitched to a painted piece of heavy watercolor paper. The watercolor piece was glued to an 8" x 10" piece of mat board, and a painted collage strip was added to the right side of the design. A wrapped chenille pipe cleaner and three air-dry clay pieces were also glued to the design. The piece was mounted inside a plastic shadowbox frame. Mat board was cut to fit along the inside edges of the shadowbox frame and painted to coordinate with the design. Three fabric motifs were glued to the edges of the frame and an air-dry clay piece was glued to the top-right edge of the frame. A stuffed doll shape, created with a black felt pen and Dye-na-Flow, was attached to the collaged background with two stacked adhesive pop-up squares. The base of the shadowbox was glued to a 1"x 4" x 10" board that was painted to coordinate with the design.

Woven Design with Collage and Embellishments

This piece is a combination of several woven pieces that have been overlapped and sewn together. The surface was embellished with machine stitching, fun-foam strips, three wrapped chenille pipe cleaners, collage, and a painted wooden shape. Kathy Hunt created the wooden shape. See "Resources" on page 110 for ordering information.

Woven Paper and Fabric Collage with Tyvek and Wrapped Pipe-Cleaner Embellishments

This is one of my favorite pieces. It combines two pieces of woven and painted watercolor paper with fabric collage. Painted and ironed Tyvek pieces and a wrapped chenille pipe cleaner add dimension to the piece. Two pieces of cardstock, wrapped with painted fabric, are adhered to the sides of the piece for additional interest.

Woven Paper and Fabric Collage with Machine Stitching and Tyvek Embellishments

For this design I created a weaving of painted watercolor paper and included thread and yarn embellishments in the weaving, allowing the ends to dangle freely. Machine stitching and Angelina embellishments were added to the piece. It was sewn to a piece of painted watercolor paper. The design was then mounted to a painted piece of illustration board, which was painted around the edges to coordinate with the design. More paint was added to the illustration board to coordinate with the design. Three painted Tyvek pieces were glued on the top right. One Tyvek piece was glued horizontally on the bottom.

RESOURCES

The Adhesive Products, Inc.
(510) 526-7616
www.craftacerspick.com
Adhesives, including Crafter's Pick The Ultimate!, Memory Mount, Fabric Glue, Batik-EZ

Clearsnap, Inc.
(360) 293-6634
www.clearsnap.com
Ancient Page and Crafter stamp pads, reinkers, Rollagraphs, Style Stones, rubber stamps, and videos

Clover Needlecraft Inc.
www.clover-use.com
Various sewing, fiber, and knitting supplies

Diane Ericson/ReVisions
(707) 540-0205
www.revisions-ericson.com
Stencils

Flights of Fancy Boutique
(800) 530-8745
www.flightsoffancyboutique.com
Embellishments and yarn

Gütermann of America
www.gutermann.com
Sewing thread

Janome America, Inc.
www.janome.com
Sewing machines for paper and fabric

Kathy Hunt
Valparaiso, Indiana
(219) 759-2887
Custom-made wooden shapes for painting and embellishments

Kretzer Scissors, Inc.
(404) 978-0062
Scissors

Lucky Squirrel
(800) 462-4912
www.luckysquirrel.com
PolyShrink shrink plastic

The Mountain Idea
www.themountainidea.com
Hearty air-dry clay, clay rollers, embellishments

Pellon
www.shoppellon.com
Wonder Under

Rainbow Silks
www.rainbowsilks.co.uk
Dyes, fabrics, yarns, papers, scrapbooking supplies, paints, books, Angelina fiber, and miscellaneous embellishments

Ranger Industries
(800) 244-2211
www.rangerink.com
Heat it Craft Tool, stamp pads, stamping and painting accessories, Cut and Dry products, bone folders, and Teflon ironing sheets

Robert Kaufman Fabrics
www.robertkaufman.com
Plain and printed fabrics, including Sherrill Kahn's fabric lines

Rupert, Gibbon & Spider
(Jacquard Products)
(800) 442-0455
www.jacquardproducts.com
Sherrill Kahn's Travel Paint Studio, Neopaque, Lumiere, Sherrill's Sorbets, Dye-na-Flow, Textile Colors, Piñata Colors, Pearl Ex stamp pads, and applicator-tipped bottles and tips

Sherrill Kahn
Impress Me Rubber Stamp Company
17116 Escalon Drive
Encino, CA 91436-4030
Telephone/Fax: (818) 788-6730
www.impressmenow.com
Catalog: $5.00, refundable with a coupon
Rubber stamps, Sherrill Kahn's Travel Paint Studio, Sherrill Kahn's books

Walnut Hollow
www.walnuthollow.com
Wooden shapes, papier-mâché forms, and various tools

Workshop on the Web
www.workshopontheweb.com
Excellent resource for projects and tips from the United Kingdom

ABOUT THE AUTHOR

Sherrill was an art educator for thirty years in the public schools with an emphasis on drawing, painting, fiber, and design. Since retirement from the public schools, she has taught nationally and internationally for stores, conferences, guilds, and educational institutions. She owns Impress Me, a rubber-stamp company, with her husband, Joel. She has four fabric lines with Robert Kaufman, paint line and paint studio products with Jacquard, and Rollagraphs and Style Stone products with Clearsnap. She has written over 40 magazine articles; this is her third book.

Sherrill has loved to draw and paint as long as she can remember. She would sit for hours coloring and painting as a young girl. She received Lincoln Logs for Christmas when she was seven and enjoyed building structures with them. She made doll clothes when she was eight using a composite doll about 9" tall with arms that were removable, so the garments could be put on and taken off easily. Her mother, Ann, who taught elementary school, taught her to sew, knit, and crochet.

Today Sherrill continues to experiment with every possible media. She loves to play endlessly with her designs on the computer, as well as draw, knit, crochet, make fused glass, and create three-dimensional pieces. Sherrill enjoys trying out every new product that seems interesting. She definitely lives by the words "What if?" and hopes you enjoy and have fun with the techniques in *Creative Embellishments*.